Springbrook School Library

S0-BNV-676

The Best Tales Ever Told
SPIRITS AND SORCERERS

Written by Stewart Ross
Illustrated by Francis Phillipps

COPPER BEECH BOOKS
BROOKFIELD, CONNECTICUT

© Aladdin Books Ltd 1998
© Text: Stewart Ross/Aladdin
Books Ltd 1998
© U.S. text 1998

Designed and produced by
Aladdin Books Ltd
28 Percy Street
London W1P 0LD

First published in
the United States in 1998 by
Copper Beech Books,
an imprint of
The Millbrook Press
2 Old New Milford Road
Brookfield, Connecticut 06804

Editor
Jim Pipe
Designed by
David West Children's Books
Designer
Simon Morse
Illustrated by
Francis Phillipps
Additional illustrations by
Ken Stott
– B.L. Kearley
Language consultant
Andrew Sharp

Printed in Belgium
All rights reserved
5 4 3 2 1

Library of Congress
Cataloging-in-Publication Data
Ross, Stewart.
Spirits and sorcerers : myths of Africa,
Egypt, and Arabia / by Stewart Ross ;
illustrated by Francis Phillipps.
p. cm. — (The best tales ever told)
Includes index.
Summary: A collection of tales from
Africa, the Middle East, and Biblical
stories from the Old Testament.
ISBN 0-7613-0709-5 (lib. bdg.)
1. Tales—Arab countries. 2. Tales—
Africa. 3. Bible stories—O.T.
[1. Folklore—Arab countries.
2. Arabs—Folklore. 3. Folklore—Africa.
4. Bible stories—O.T.] I. Phillipps,
Francis, ill. II. Title. III. Series.
PZ8.1.R692Kn 1998   97-41200
398.2—dc21   CIP AC

CONTENTS

4 DAVID and GOLIATH
What chance does shorty
have against mighty Goliath?

6 ALADDIN and the MAGIC LAMP
One rub and Aladdin can have
anything his heart desires.

8 ISIS collects her HUSBAND
Isis searches far and wide when
her husband is ripped apart.

10 JALIYA and the RIVER GOD
What lurks in the murky gray-
green waters of the Gongola?

12 LITTLE MAN and the MUNCHING MONSTER
Can Little Man rescue the
valley from the greedy giant?

14 ALI BABA and the FORTY THIEVES
Who can save Ali Baba
from the ruthless thieves?

16 NOAH and the ARK
Who can stand the smell
after two weeks at sea?

18 THE LION GODDESS
What do you do when your
baby starts growing claws?

20 SAMSON and DELILAH
Will Delilah find out the
secret of Samson's strength?

22 SCHEHEREZADE
How can telling tales keep
the executioner waiting?

24 SOLOMON and SHEBA
What happens when two
brainboxes fight it out?

26 SINBAD and the OLD MAN of the SEA
Why does Sinbad never
give a lift to strangers?

28 TRICKY TERMS

29 WHO'S WHO

32 INDEX

INTRODUCTION

THESE TWELVE STORIES are some of the most famous ever told. Most come from the Middle East, where the Jews and Arabs have lived for thousands of years. The rest come from Africa.

Isis Collects Her Husband comes from ancient Egypt and is one of the world's oldest stories. The other African tales were written down only in modern times. Before that, they were passed on by word of mouth. The stories of the Jews (also known as the Israelites) are found in the Old Testament, the Hebrew Bible. From the Jews, the tales passed on to Christians and Muslims and spread all over the world.

The Arab tales were gathered from India and Iran (Persia) as well as Arabia, and were written down in the Arabic language. The most famous collection of stories from this part of the world is *The Arabian Nights*. It includes stories about Sinbad, Ali Baba, and Aladdin and his Magic Lamp.

People told stories for fun and to try and make sense of things they didn't understand. The story of Noah, for example, may have been based on a flood that happened thousands of years ago. Most of the tales also have a moral — they were told to teach people how to behave. All these stories have changed a lot over the centuries. To help you, we have picked out the best parts and made them easy to understand. We hope you'll enjoy them as much as those who first heard them many, many years ago.

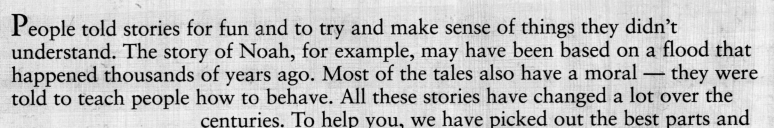

> *A Guide to Tongue-Twisting*
> Some old names can be tricky to say. To make it easier for you, we have broken down long names into smaller parts.
> For example, Osiris should be said "oh-<u>sire</u>-is." The underlining shows where to say the word louder. So with Osiris, say the "<u>sire</u>" a bit louder than the rest.

DAVID *and* GOLIATH

"DAVID!" Jesse's voice carried far into the hills through the hot, still air. "David! You're wanted." "Coming, dad!" the boy shouted back. As nimble as a mountain goat, he leapt down the slope. "What's up, dad?" he asked when he got to the house.

The Sheperd King
The real shepherd boy David, who died about 1000 B.C., went on to become the greatest king the Israelites (Jews) had ever had.

Jesse smiled. "Leave the sheep for a while and take lunch over to your brothers in the army. They'll be starving by now." David punched the air. "Cool! Thanks, dad!" He grabbed the food and jogged off down the road. "Remember, son," Jesse called after him, "no fighting! You're too young!"

Tall Guys
The Bible says that Goliath was 9.5 feet tall, but this is probably an exaggeration. At 8.9 feet, Robert Wadlow was the tallest person of modern times: by the age of 11, he was already 6.4 feet tall!

David found the Israelite (*is-rail-light*) army on one side of the Elah Valley. Their enemies, the Philistines, stood facing them on the other side. David was just about to ask why there wasn't any fighting, when the biggest guy he'd ever seen stepped out from the enemy lines.

"Listen, Israelites!" he bellowed in a voice like thunder. "What's the point of a battle? Send out your best soldier to fight me, one to one. If he kills me, we'll surrender. But if I kill him, then you'll surrender. Got it?"

The Israelites shuffled their feet and looked embarrassed. David couldn't believe it. "What's the matter?" he asked. "Why doesn't someone fight him?" "Oh yeah?" said his eldest brother. "Like who? You want to take on a great bruiser like Goliath?" David looked surprised. "Why not? The bigger they are, the harder they fall."

Before his brothers could stop him, David called across the valley, "Hang on, Goliath! I'll fight you!" Soon, armed only with his trusty sling, he was walking calmly down to meet the giant.

Super Slings
The biggest slings ever made were medieval machines called trebuchets (tray-boo-shays). These threw huge stones to smash castle walls.

"You must be joking!" roared Goliath when he saw him. "Is this the best the Israelites can come up with? Come here, squirt, so I can step on you!"

David didn't reply. He chose five smooth stones from a stream, fitted one into his sling, and watched the giant lumbering toward him. Fifty paces, thirty paces... Suddenly the shepherd boy swung his sling and let fly the stone. His aim was true — and deadly. The stone landed with a sickening thud slap in the middle of the giant's forehead. His eyes went blurry, his knees buckled, and he crashed to the ground. Dead!

David grabbed Goliath's sword and cut off his head. The Israelite army let out a loud cheer. David's brothers ran up. "Wow, David!" they panted. "How did you do it?" "No problem," David smiled. "The bigger they are, the harder they fall."

Holy Crooks
Shepherds were important to many ancient peoples as their flocks provided food and clothing. They used crooks, poles with hooks on the end, for catching sheep's legs. Christian bishops still carry crooks as a sign that they are shepherds of their people.

ALADDIN *and the* MAGIC LAMP

BESIDE THE DUSTY AFRICAN DESERT lived the cleverest sorcerer ever. For forty years he worked with spells and magic potions until — at last! — he discovered the world's greatest secret. Far away, hidden in a dark Chinese cave, lay a vast treasure and a magic lamp.

Caravan Routes
Hundreds of years ago, people often made the journey to and from Arabia and China. Lines of camels, known as caravans, carried silk and spices thousands of miles across Asia.

The sorcerer found out that only a young boy named Aladdin could find the treasure and the lamp, so he took off to China to track him down. After he'd found the boy the sorcerer took him to the cave and told him that if he brought out the old lamp, he'd be as rich as a king.

Evil Genies
In Arab myth, as well as helpful genies, there were evil ones who picked up innocent women and carried them off.

With a flash the sorcerer opened the cave and in Aladdin went. The boy found the lamp, but he collected so many jewels he couldn't climb out again. This made the sorcerer really mad. With another flash he closed the cave, trapping Aladdin inside.

Aladdin sat there for a while, then started rubbing the lamp to clean it. ZAP! A huge genie stood before him. "Hello, sir!" it cried. "What can I do for you today?"

Being a bright boy, Aladdin soon figured out the lamp was magic and the genie would do anything he wanted. He got it to carry him out of the cave and build him a beautiful palace, full of gold, jewels, servants, and candy. Even better, when the Emperor of China heard about Aladdin's amazing palace, he let him marry his only daughter, the husky Bedr-al-Budur (*bad-rall* boo-*derr*).

Ancient Learning — or Magic?

To people in the past, there was little difference between science and magic. For example, in the tale of Aladdin (whose name should really be said "al-lah-ah-deen"), the sorcerer learns where Aladdin is by studying the stars. In Arab myths, sorcerers often come from North Africa. This may be because the North African town of Timbuktu, in Mali, was a center of learning (left), with its own university.

Sandy Jokers
Desert peoples believed sudden sandstorms were blown up by annoying genies.

Meanwhile, the sorcerer used his magic to see what had happened to the lamp. When he saw it in Aladdin's palace, he bought a dozen new lamps and wandered about calling, "New lamps for old!" One morning, when her husband was out, the beautiful Bedr-al-Budur heard the cry and, not knowing Aladdin's lamp was magic, she swapped it for a new one.

Immediately the sorcerer got the genie to carry Aladdin's palace, with Badr-al-Budur inside, deep into the African desert. When Aladdin came back to where his palace had been, he soon figured out what had happened and also left for Africa. After a long search, he found his palace and got in touch with Bedr-al-Budur.

The poor girl was in a real state because the sorcerer was pestering her to marry him. Aladdin gave her some deadly poison and, pretending to really like the sorcerer, she poured it into his wine and killed him. So in the end Aladdin got his lamp back, Bedr-al-Budur got her husband back — and the greedy sorcerer got what he deserved.

ISIS *collects her* HUSBAND

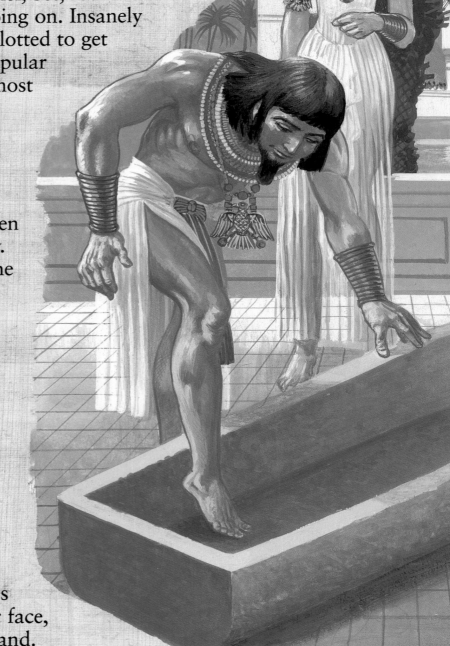

Just after everything had begun, the Earth god and the Sky goddess set up Osiris (*oh-sire-is*) and Isis as king and queen of Egypt. They made a great pair. Not only were they crazy about each other, but they helped all the other Egyptians by teaching them about religion and farming.

Animal Mummies
Animals associated with the ancient Egyptian gods and goddesses were mummified like humans when they died — including cats, birds, and crocodiles!

All this was fine until King Osiris' wicked brother, Set, found out what was going on. Insanely jealous, he plotted to get rid of the popular king in the most horrible way he could think of. He secretly measured Osiris and had a beautiful coffin made exactly his size, with gold paint and carvings.

Next, Set invited the king and queen and all the top Egyptians to a party. When they'd all had a good meal, he showed them the coffin and said it was a present for whoever it fitted.

The Egyptians just loved a good coffin and all the guests lay down in Set's box to see if it was their size. Of course, only Osiris fitted perfectly. As soon as he was in, Set's servants nailed down the lid, covered the coffin in lead, and chucked it into the Nile River.

Poor Queen Isis! She cut off her long hair, dressed in widow's clothes and, with tears streaming down her face, set off to look for her missing husband.

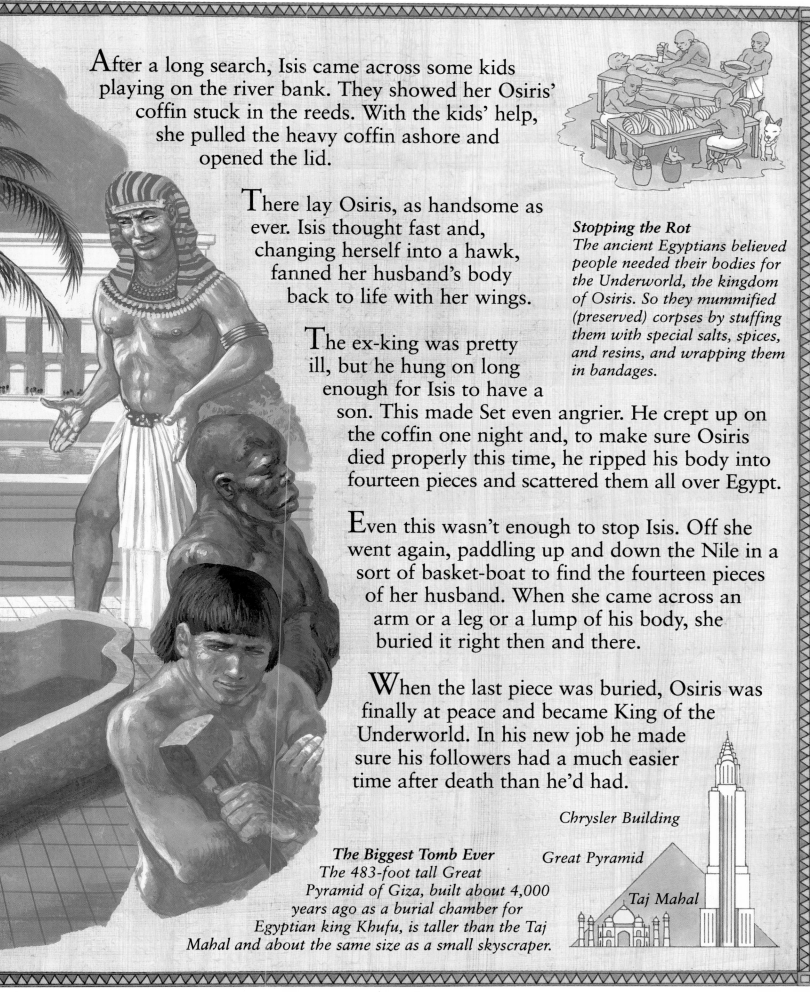

After a long search, Isis came across some kids playing on the river bank. They showed her Osiris' coffin stuck in the reeds. With the kids' help, she pulled the heavy coffin ashore and opened the lid.

There lay Osiris, as handsome as ever. Isis thought fast and, changing herself into a hawk, fanned her husband's body back to life with her wings.

Stopping the Rot
The ancient Egyptians believed people needed their bodies for the Underworld, the kingdom of Osiris. So they mummified (preserved) corpses by stuffing them with special salts, spices, and resins, and wrapping them in bandages.

The ex-king was pretty ill, but he hung on long enough for Isis to have a son. This made Set even angrier. He crept up on the coffin one night and, to make sure Osiris died properly this time, he ripped his body into fourteen pieces and scattered them all over Egypt.

Even this wasn't enough to stop Isis. Off she went again, paddling up and down the Nile in a sort of basket-boat to find the fourteen pieces of her husband. When she came across an arm or a leg or a lump of his body, she buried it right then and there.

When the last piece was buried, Osiris was finally at peace and became King of the Underworld. In his new job he made sure his followers had a much easier time after death than he'd had.

Chrysler Building

Great Pyramid

Taj Mahal

The Biggest Tomb Ever
The 483-foot tall Great Pyramid of Giza, built about 4,000 years ago as a burial chamber for Egyptian king Khufu, is taller than the Taj Mahal and about the same size as a small skyscraper.

JALIYA *and the* RIVER GOD

VILLAGE GIRLS often teased the beautiful Jaliya. Down on the bank of the Gongola River, they crowded around and pushed her toward the river. "Jaliya is a creep! Push her in the deep!" they chanted. Then someone gave an extra hard push and Jaliya toppled into the water.

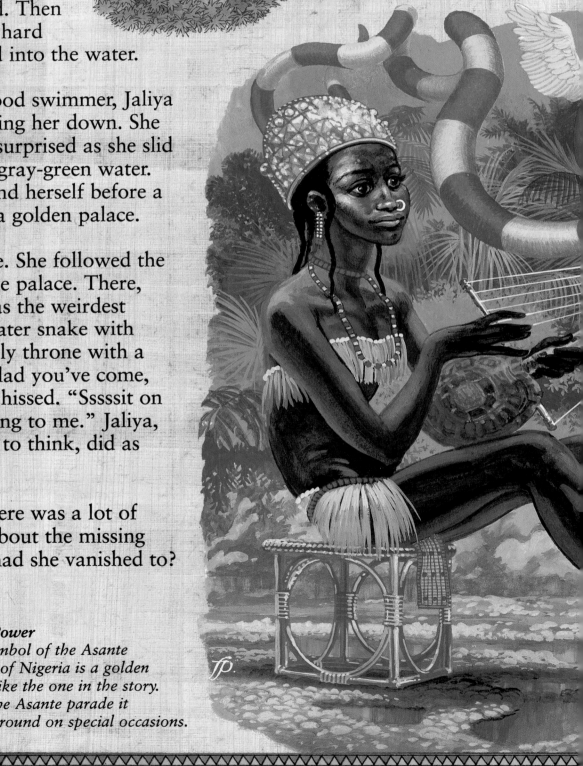

Big Splash
The 5,576-foot wide Victoria Falls on the Zambezi River are Africa's most spectacular natural water works.

Although she was a good swimmer, Jaliya felt a strange force pulling her down. She wasn't frightened, just surprised as she slid peacefully through the gray-green water. On the bottom she found herself before a line of trees leading to a golden palace.

Jaliya set off to explore. She followed the line of trees down to the palace. There, right in front of her, was the weirdest sight ever: a gigantic water snake with wings, sitting on a pearly throne with a crown on his head! "Glad you've come, Jaliya," the snake-king hissed. "Ssssit on that sssssstool and sssssing to me." Jaliya, who didn't know what to think, did as she was told.

Back on the surface there was a lot of wailing and moaning about the missing girl. Where had she vanished to?

Stool Power
The symbol of the Asante people of Nigeria is a golden stool, like the one in the story. The Asante parade it around on special occasions.

10

A few days later, the village chief was wandering along the bank of the Gongola thinking about the drowned girl, when he heard a sort of faint singing. The villagers thought he was a bit crazy, but because he was chief they did what he said.

They built a clay dam across the river, just above where Jaliya had fallen in. When most of the water had drained away, the snake-king took off in a cloud of steam and flapped away to find a deeper pool. Then the bottom came into sight, and there was Jaliya! She was wearing a golden crown, sitting on a golden stool, and playing a golden harp.

What a Header!
Most societies have special headgear for their important people, but not many are as fantastic as this Chinese crown!

The chief thought she was the neatest thing he'd ever seen. Not caring about his fancy clothes, he jumped down into the mud and carried her to the bank. "Well?" he gasped. "What happened?"

Jaliya told him about her adventure and explained that the snake-king (who was really the river god) had made her queen of the river. He'd also given her lots of gold and precious things. "Do you think a village chief could marry a river queen?" the chief asked nervously.

Jaliya smiled at him. "Why not? The river god said I could live on land, as long as I throw a big present into the river for him once a year." "No problem," replied the chief. "It's worth staying on his good side — We don't want to lose you again, do we?"

The Ultimate Present
Many ancient peoples offered presents to their gods. In Europe, Celtic priests, known as druids, gave their gods the ultimate sacrifice — human beings!

LITTLE MAN *and the* MUNCHING MONSTER

IT WAS ONE OF THE GREENEST, shadiest, happiest valleys in all Africa. Every family had a neat little hut. Their fields grew all the food they needed, chickens scratched in the yards, and fat cattle grazed in the meadows. Visitors called it a dreamland.

Then the terrible munching monster turned up and ruined everything. It came into the valley down a narrow rocky road through the mountains, sniffed around a bit, and started eating. It ate every living thing it could find: people, animals, trees, plants — even wasps and ants. By late afternoon there was nothing left, except one pregnant woman.

Belly Travel
The most famous swallowing story is Jonah and the Giant Whale. After three days and nights in the whale's belly, Jonah jumped out alive onto the beach. Some historians think the whale may have been a great white shark.

Seeing the monster slurping toward her, she pretended to be a stone. The beast was pretty full by now and didn't want anything more to eat, not even a meaty-smelling stone. So it turned back up the narrow road and tried to get out of the valley. But it was so fat, it got stuck between the rocks.

What a Mouthful!
Boas, anacondas, and pythons swallow their victims whole, just like the monster in the story, but crush them to death first. Deer, leopards, and even crocodiles have been found in the stomachs of these huge snakes.

All this was such a shock for the woman that she gave birth to a baby son, right then and there. Then she went to get a drink, but when she came back her baby was gone and a man was standing where it had been. "Hello!" she said anxiously. "Have you seen a baby lying around?" The man smiled. "Don't worry, mom. I'm your baby. I've just grown up a bit quick, that's all." The woman called her baby Little Man and told him about the Munching Monster. "I'll be back soon, mom!" he cried, grabbing a knife and running off up the road.

The monster growled and howled when it saw Little Man coming, but it was stuck too tight to do anything. Little Man put his ear to its stomach. "Just in time!" he muttered. With a swish of his knife he cut the monster open and WOOOSH — out came everything it had swallowed — even the wasps and ants! Little Man had saved the valley! Soon the plants and crops were growing again and everyone was feeling great. Well, not quite everyone.

Ready for Action
Mythical people like Little Man and Merlin, King Arthur's wizard, grew amazingly quickly into adults. In nature, the babies of some tree frogs leap fully-formed from the adult's pouch.

One survivor, who had been hurt when Little Man sliced open the monster, hated the little hero and plotted to kill him. He tried ambush after ambush, but each time, Little Man easily escaped. In the end, however, Little Man got so fed up with all the hassle he just stood there and let his enemy chop his head off. His mom was shattered. "You see," she sobbed. "Some people are never grateful, no matter what you do for them."

ALI BABA *and the* FORTY THIEVES

BAGHDAD WAS RICH like no other city. Its stalls glistened with jewels, its markets jostled with merchants, and its gold lit up the night sky.

But wealth brings thieves. Ali Baba, like all Baghdad merchants, knew this only too well, so when he was returning home one evening and noticed shady figures on the road ahead, he dived into the shadows. Creeping forward, he spied a band of forty thieves, each carrying a bag of loot.

As Ali watched, the thieves left the road and went up to a rock. "Open sesame!" whispered their leader. Immediately, a door opened and the gang disappeared inside. Ten minutes later they came out again — without their bags.

When they were gone, Ali crept up to the rock. "Open sesame!" he muttered. The door opened and he found himself in the bandits' lair, stacked to the roof with sacks of stolen treasure. "Wow!" he whooped. Grabbing as much as he could carry, he opened the door with the password and ran home. He did this every day, until the cave was empty and he was a very rich man.

Let me in!
"Open Sesame" is the world's most famous password. Today, passwords are still used by soldiers on guard to check out whether strangers are friend or foe.

A Dangerous Business
Treasure hunting was not just the stuff of legend. One Arab tomb robber even wrote a manual warning about such dangers as sword-carrying statues, trip wires, and collapsing staircases.

When they found their loot gone, the thieves went wild and their leader organized a search of every building in the city. As they checked a house, they marked the door with chalk. The marks got closer and closer to Ali's house.

Ali had told only his servant girl, Morgana, what he had done. Out shopping one day, she noticed the suspicious chalk marks and put one on her master's door. This fooled the thieves, who figured out their mistake only after checking every house in Baghdad!

Sinister Stronghold
The Assassins, who built huge castles in remote areas of Iran, were the deadliest of all Muslim gangs. We get the word "assassinate" from their murderous deeds.

The bandit leader now knew Ali was his target. He pretended to be an oil merchant and bought forty huge jars. With a thief hiding in each one, they were delivered to Ali's house. The thieves planned to jump out at night, kill the whole household, and make off with the loot.

Ali didn't suspect a thing. But when the sharp-eyed Morgana noticed a turban sticking out of one of the jars, she quickly understood what was going on. Oil jars are for oil, she decided. So oil is what they'll get. She boiled up a big pot of it and filled each jar to the brim.

That was the end of the forty thieves. Ali Baba's treasures were safe and he rewarded the reliable Morgana by letting her marry his handsome son — which was only fair, considering she had saved his money and his life.

Cunning Kitty
Myths and legends are full of crafty servants saving their masters by their cleverness and skill. The storybook character Puss-in-Boots, who helps his master become rich and famous, comes from a 16th-century Italian tale.

NOAH *and the* ARK

NOT LONG AFTER GOD had made the world, he decided things weren't quite right. The plants grew just fine and the animals wandered happily around doing animal-type things. The problem was the people!

God had planned them to be happy and well-behaved. Instead, they swore, bullied, stole, fought, and were generally revolting. So God decided to get rid of the whole lot and start again. Before he did so, he checked once more in case he'd missed someone truly good. That's when he noticed Noah. God could hardly believe it: Not only was Noah incredibly old (about 600), but he was also incredibly good. He didn't get angry, he worked hard, and he always cleaned his ancient teeth. "Ahem! Noah!" God whispered. "It's me, God, calling."

A Raft of Myth
According to the myths of the Hopi people of America, during a great flood people were saved by building a huge raft.

Noah had never spoken to God before. "W-what do you want, Lord?" he stuttered nervously. "Listen, Noah. I'm so fed up with everyone misbehaving, I'm going to drown the lot. But I'll save you, your family, and all the animals. So build an ENORMOUS boat, and get yourselves and two of every creature aboard. It's going to rain like never before, so hurry up."

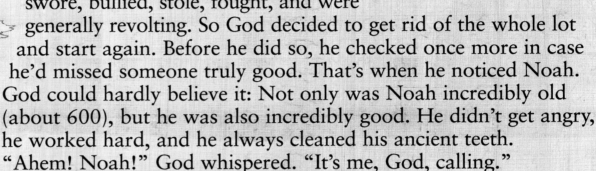

Dino-Disaster
In the 19th century, some people believed that dinosaurs had died out because Noah hadn't taken them into the Ark!

Golden Oldies
Better diet and medical care mean that people are living longer and longer. But there's a long way to go before anyone beats Noah!

Noah knew God wasn't a joker and he started building right away. The Ark was so big he had to knock down his house to make room for it. The neighbors said he was crazy. They laughed even more when he got Mrs. Noah, their three sons, and their wives to help him round up the animals.

Rain of Terror
The tale of Noah and his Ark may come from the flood stories of the ancient Sumerian people.

Their tales were based on memories of real floods along the mighty Euphrates River (you-fray-tees) that washed away whole towns.

Then it started raining. The ditches swelled the streams, the streams grew to rivers, and the rivers flooded the whole countryside. Noah's neighbors realized he wasn't so crazy after all. "Hey Noah! Let us in!" they cried, pounding on the side of the Ark.

Noah poked his head out. "Sorry folks! God said no passengers!" So the flood rose, covering the whole Earth, and everyone was drowned.

When it finally stopped raining and the flood went down a bit, Noah sent a dove to find dry land. Half an hour later it came back with an olive branch in its beak. "Yipee!" yelled Noah. "Land ahoy! Steer north, Mrs. Noah!"

The Ark touched down on Mount Ararat. When the flood had gone down a bit more, Noah let out all the animals. Soon afterward, he followed with his family, ready to start their lives over again. "And remember," Noah said seriously, "only smiles and good manners this time!"

The LION GODDESS

NYAVIREZI (*un-yah-veer-ay-zee*), THE CHIEF'S DAUGHTER, loved wandering around the countryside on her own. She didn't know why, but she felt freer and more relaxed out in the wild. The sights, sounds, and smells of nature made her feel really alive.

Deadlier than the Male
Although we think of the lion as the King of Beasts, the smaller lioness is more fierce — especially when protecting her young. The lioness also does most of the hunting.

One day she went farther than usual and by midday she was very thirsty. Finding water in a hollow tree, she drank and turned for home. Unbeknown to her, however, the water had been put there by a lioness.

As the girl approached her village, she saw her father's cattle quietly grazing in the fields. Wow, they looked good! So fat and juicy and… before she knew what was happening, Nyavirezi changed into a huge lioness. Bounding up to the largest cow, she killed and ate it. She then changed back to a girl and walked into the village.

After this had happened a few times, her father grew suspicious. He followed her on one of her walks, saw her change into a lioness, and banned her from going out ever again.

A year or two later, Nyavirezi married a chief from a neighboring village and had a baby son. Her husband was as proud as a peacock until, one afternoon, he heard his wife's servants whispering together over the baby's crib.

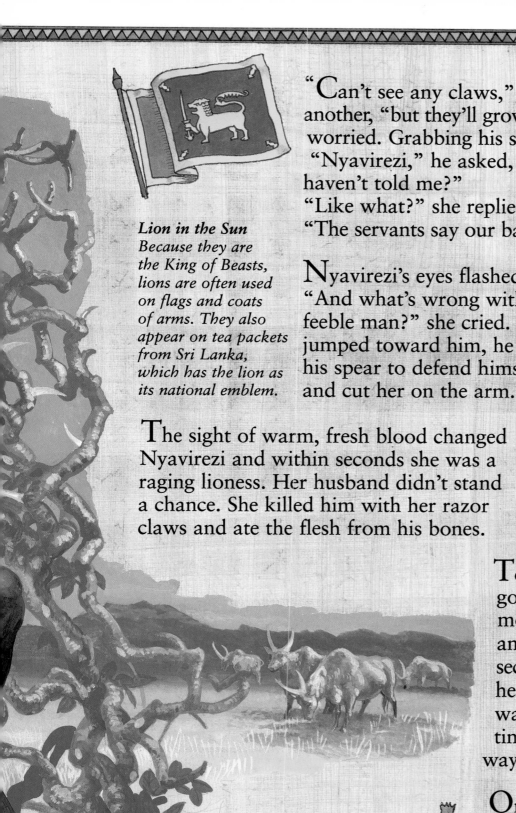

"Can't see any claws," said one. "Not yet," said another, "but they'll grow soon enough." The chief was worried. Grabbing his spear, he went to find his wife. "Nyavirezi," he asked, "is there something you haven't told me?"

"Like what?" she replied, looking angry.

"The servants say our baby's going to grow claws."

Lion in the Sun
Because they are the King of Beasts, lions are often used on flags and coats of arms. They also appear on tea packets from Sri Lanka, which has the lion as its national emblem.

Nyavirezi's eyes flashed with fury. "And what's wrong with that, you feeble man?" she cried. As she jumped toward him, he lifted his spear to defend himself and cut her on the arm.

The sight of warm, fresh blood changed Nyavirezi and within seconds she was a raging lioness. Her husband didn't stand a chance. She killed him with her razor claws and ate the flesh from his bones.

Lofty Lookouts
East African lions fear just one sound — the bells of Masai cattle. The giant Masai people are great hunters as well as herders, and their height helps them, literally, to watch over their herds.

To get away from all the nasty gossip about her, Nyavirezi moved to a village far away and married again. In time her second husband found out about her changes but kept quiet. She was a good wife — most of the time — and he kept out of the way when she went on the prowl.

Out of Africa
Many of the world's most famous legends, such as the story of the race between the hare and the tortoise, originally came from Africa.

One night, however, Nyavirezi went out and never returned. No one went to look for her. They knew that Nyavirezi, the Lion Goddess, had finally returned to the wild where she belonged.

SAMSON *and* DELILAH

A COUPLE OF MISERABLE PHILISTINE soldiers huddled around their campfire. Not long ago they had the Israelites beaten. Now, because of just one man, everything had changed.

Too Big for his Boots?
The ancient Greek wrestler Milon loved showing off by carrying a bull on his shoulders. But when he split a tree with his bare hands, one hand got stuck, and he was eaten by a pack of wolves.

"Kill Samson!" cried one soldier. "What chance do we have against that great Israelite thug?"

His friend grunted. "Samson wasted a thousand of us yesterday. It's like fighting a mad elephant."

The first Philistine stared into the fire. "He's got one weakness, you know," he said slowly. "Oh yeah?"

"Women."

The second Philistine suddenly jumped to his feet. "That's it!" he cried. "Come on, let's go and see that Delilah (*de-lie-la*). I bet she'll help us."

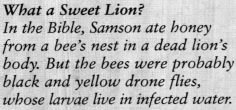

What a Sweet Lion?
In the Bible, Samson ate honey from a bee's nest in a dead lion's body. But the bees were probably black and yellow drone flies, whose larvae live in infected water.

Long or Short?
The length of people's hair can tell us something about them. In the 1960s, hippies had long hair to show their freedom, while soldiers have crewcuts to show their discipline.

Delilah, Samson's girlfriend, loved her hunky hero, but she loved money a lot more. So when the Philistines offered her a fortune to find out the secret of Samson's strength, she agreed to help. "Samson darling," she sighed next time they met, "why are you so strong?"

The muscle man had promised God not to tell anyone the secret of his strength. "Tie me up with new string," he joked, "and I'll be as weak as a kitten." Delilah tried this, but Samson brushed away the string as if it were a spider's web. The next time Delilah asked, Samson told her to try new rope. That didn't work either. The third time Delilah asked, Samson said, "Braid my hair, honey, and see what that does to my strength." It made no difference at all.

Delilah was getting desperate. "Please, Samson," she begged, "if you really love me, tell me the secret of your strength." Though he felt bad about it, Samson finally gave in. "OK. You win, Delilah. Cut off my hair and I'll be as feeble as a fly."

Delilah gave him a big kiss and he fell asleep. The Philistines then shaved his head while he was sleeping and when he woke up, his strength was gone. His enemies blinded him and led him away in chains to prison.

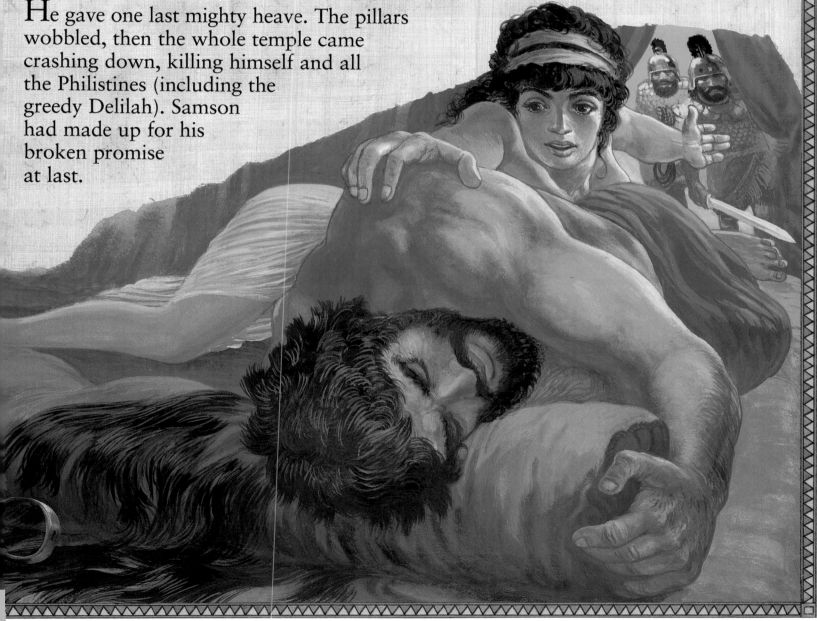

Months later, the Philistines held a feast to honor their god, Dagon. Hundreds of them piled into the temple and shouted for Samson to be brought in. When the ex-hero appeared, dirty and miserable, the Philistines hooted with laughter.

Samson asked the jailer if he could put his hands on the temple pillars to rest. The jailer agreed, forgetting Samson's hair had grown back. He was now as strong as ever.

Super Strong
Every country has its own legends of super-strong men. The Indian hero Bhima was famous for tearing apart gorilla monsters with his bare hands.

He gave one last mighty heave. The pillars wobbled, then the whole temple came crashing down, killing himself and all the Philistines (including the greedy Delilah). Samson had made up for his broken promise at last.

SCHEHEREZADE

RIDING BACK TO HIS PALACE, King Shahriar (*shar-ree-yar*) felt pretty pleased with himself. His kingdom was large, rich, and spicy. As he passed by, his people bowed down in terror and respect. It's neat to be king, he thought.

Nearing his palace, he decided to surprise his lovely wife, Shahriala (*shah-ree-al-lah*). He plucked a rose and ran up the stairs into her room. "Hello, my angel!" he cried. "I'm home!"

Shahriala, however, was not pleased to see him — she was in the arms of her favorite slave! Wild with fury, the king drew his sword and killed them both before they even had time to apologize.

The king shut himself in his room and refused to eat or speak for a week. When he came out, pale and hard-eyed, he called for his chief advisor. "All women are wicked," he snarled. "For revenge, bring me a fresh wife!"

The advisor hurried off and came back ten minutes later with a pretty new bride. The king married her right away. At breakfast the next morning, Shahriar called for his advisor. "This girl does not please me," he snarled. "Strangle her and bring me another."

The chief advisor blinked. "Did you say "strangle her," your majesty?" "I did!" snapped Shahriar. "Now get on with it, unless you want to be strangled yourself."

Take Your Pick!
In some countries a man is allowed several wives — but only if he can afford to look after them and promises to treat them all equally.

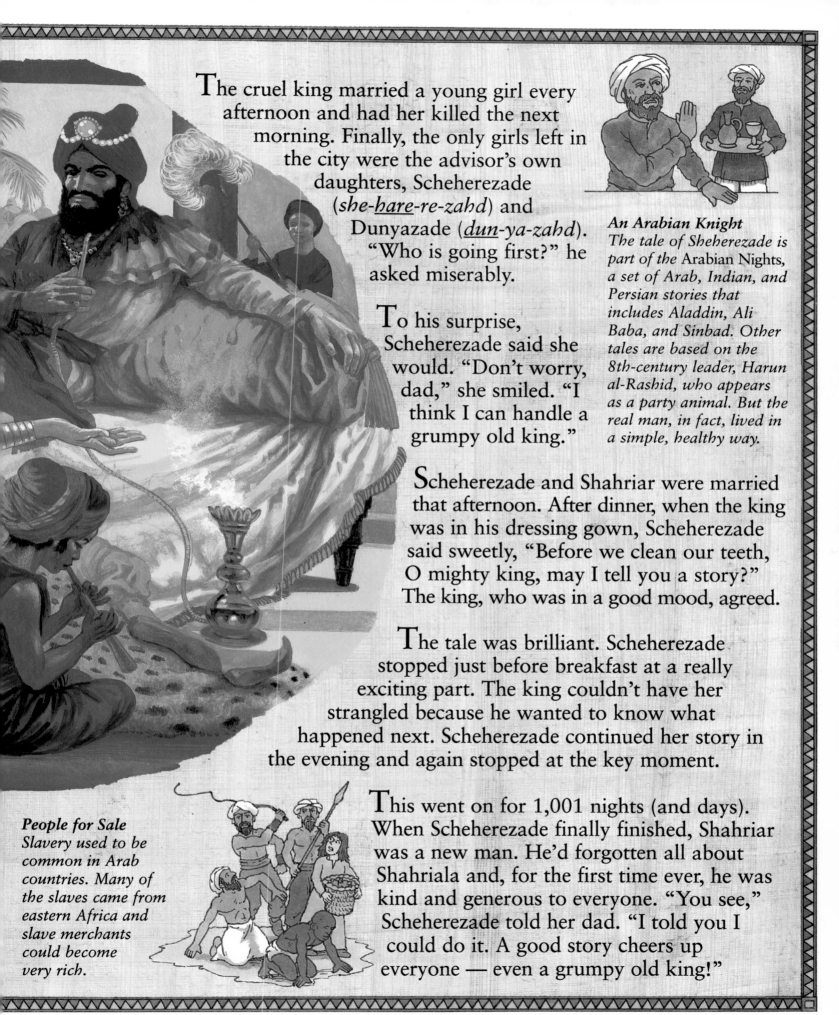

The cruel king married a young girl every afternoon and had her killed the next morning. Finally, the only girls left in the city were the advisor's own daughters, Scheherezade (*she-hare-re-zahd*) and Dunyazade (*dun-ya-zahd*). "Who is going first?" he asked miserably.

To his surprise, Scheherezade said she would. "Don't worry, dad," she smiled. "I think I can handle a grumpy old king."

An Arabian Knight
The tale of Sheherezade is part of the Arabian Nights, a set of Arab, Indian, and Persian stories that includes Aladdin, Ali Baba, and Sinbad. Other tales are based on the 8th-century leader, Harun al-Rashid, who appears as a party animal. But the real man, in fact, lived in a simple, healthy way.

Scheherezade and Shahriar were married that afternoon. After dinner, when the king was in his dressing gown, Scheherezade said sweetly, "Before we clean our teeth, O mighty king, may I tell you a story?" The king, who was in a good mood, agreed.

The tale was brilliant. Scheherezade stopped just before breakfast at a really exciting part. The king couldn't have her strangled because he wanted to know what happened next. Scheherezade continued her story in the evening and again stopped at the key moment.

People for Sale
Slavery used to be common in Arab countries. Many of the slaves came from eastern Africa and slave merchants could become very rich.

This went on for 1,001 nights (and days). When Scheherezade finally finished, Shahriar was a new man. He'd forgotten all about Shahriala and, for the first time ever, he was kind and generous to everyone. "You see," Scheherezade told her dad. "I told you I could do it. A good story cheers up everyone — even a grumpy old king!"

SOLOMON *and* SHEBA

IN VERY ANCIENT TIMES, long before automobiles and telescopes, the Israelites believed their King Solomon was the greatest. Not only was he rich and strong, he was also as wise as a whole flock of owls.

One of the cleverest things he ever did was sort out the question: "Who is the true mother." Two squabbling women came to him with a baby. "It's mine!" wailed the green-eyed woman. "No, it's mine!" sobbed the other woman, who had brown eyes.

Solomon noticed the baby had one green eye and one brown eye. "What a shame!" he said sadly, "I'll have to cut the baby in two and give you each a half." The brown-eyed woman agreed. But the green-eyed woman burst into tears because she didn't want the baby killed. Solomon gave her the baby, because she obviously loved it more than the other woman.

Not far away lived Balkis, Queen of Sheba. She was also very clever, and when she heard about all the neat things Solomon did, she wrote and said she was coming to visit him. She wanted to see if he was as brainy as her. Solomon was a little worried when he got her letter, because he'd heard Balkis was a bit of a witch.

Law Man
The story of Solomon and the baby shows how in ancient times kings had to be "jacks-of-all-trades" — not just soldiers and rulers, but judges as well.

Mystery Millions
Legends of King Solomon's wealth spread throughout Africa. In the 19th century, greedy European explorers searched in vain for his hidden treasure.

The real giveaway with witches was their hairy legs. To test Balkis, Solomon had mirror tiles laid in the hall of his palace. So when she walked in, he glanced down and saw her legs in the mirrors on the floor. Not a hair on them! He breathed a huge sigh of relief.

The Sun Queen
The real Balkis came from Yemen in southwestern Arabia. Her people worshiped the brightest and most powerful thing they knew — the Sun!

Balkis stayed with Solomon for days, testing him with tricky questions about the stars, religion, geography, history, math, and so on. He always got everything correct! Balkis was just as sharp and answered all Solomon's quizzes, no problem.

When it was time for Balkis to go back to Sheba, the king and queen met in the hall with the mirror tiles to say goodbye. Balkis looked down at the floor. "Nice try, Solomon," she smiled.

The king looked embarrassed. "I just wanted to check your legs," he explained. "You know what some people say about you." Balkis nodded. "So, do you think that I am a witch?"
"No way!" Solomon laughed. "You're just the cleverest woman ever!"
"And you're the cleverest fellow ever," replied Balkis, "so let's call it quits."

Solomon agreed. It was a really sensible thing to do and it proved that, when it came to brains, Solomon and Balkis were quite equal in the whole world!

The African Sheba
Balkis was also known to the Ethiopians, who called her Eteye Azeba, "Queen of the South." In their myths, she was rescued from a fire-breathing dragon by seven Christian saints.

SINBAD *and the* OLD MAN *of the* SEA

THE BRASS PLATE OUTSIDE Sinbad's house in Baghdad read "Sinbad the Merchant." But everyone knew of him as Sinbad the Sailor, because he was always off on voyages of adventure.

On one voyage Sinbad's crews went ashore on an island to collect water. There, half-buried in the sand, they saw an enormous white dome. Sinbad recognized an egg of the gigantic roc bird and warned them to get out — fast!

Bucket Beak
The roc was perhaps based on the Sudanese whale-headed stork which grows 4.3 feet tall and has a beak as big as a bucket!
The huge prehistoric diatryma bird (above) was over 6.4 feet tall!

But the crew laughed at him and threw rocks at the egg until it broke. They heaved out the baby roc and roasted it over a fire. As they were finishing their feast, the black shadow of the mother roc blotted out the sun. Terrified, everyone ran back to the ship and made for the open sea.

The monster bird picked up an enormous boulder in its claws and bombed them, smashing the ship to pieces. Those who weren't killed by the boulder swam for their lives.

Sinbad clung to a piece of wood and drifted to another island. It was a beautiful place, with massive fruit trees, babbling brooks, and banks of sweet-smelling wildflowers. After drying himself in the sun, Sinbad set off to explore.

Globe Trotter
Real-life Arab explorer Ibn Battuta went on an amazing 30-year journey (1325–1355) from North Africa to China! No doubt he brought back stories of terrifying sea monsters that got better with each telling.

Where Am I?
Arab sailors used an astrolabe, an early instrument to work out the position of the sun or stars. This helped them find out where they were.

On a grassy mound before a stream he found a weird old man dressed in leaves. He didn't reply when Sinbad spoke to him, but he made gestures indicating that he wanted to be carried over the stream. Taking pity on the wrinkled old man, Sinbad hoisted him onto his shoulders and ferried him across.

When Sinbad stooped to let the old man off, however, he refused to budge! The merchant jumped and shook, but this only made the old man grip even tighter.

Poor Sinbad carried the skinny old brute around the island for weeks, stopping only to sleep and let him pick fruit. Then the crafty sailor had a bright idea. He plucked some grapes and crushed the juice into a large shell. Returning a few days later, he found the juice had turned to wine.

The old man immediately grabbed the shell and gulped down the wine. Five minutes later, he started swaying and, too drunk to hold on, he tumbled to the ground. Sinbad seized his chance. Picking up a stone, he bashed the bully's brains out.

A few days later, Sinbad was rescued by a passing ship. When the captain heard about his adventure, he said the merchant was the only person he knew who'd escaped from the terrible Old Man of the Sea. "You're not only the luckiest sailor ever, Sinbad," he laughed, "but also the craftiest!"

Rotten Luck
Sinbad was saved by one of human beings' earliest discoveries — when grape juice is left to rot ("ferment") it turns into wine!

27

TRICKY TERMS

All words in capitals, e.g. SOULS, have their own explanation.

Bible
The Bible is the most SACRED book of the Jewish and Christian religions. However, Jews accept only the first part, the Old Testament, which describes the history and religion of ancient Palestine (part of which is now the modern country of Israel).

Immortal
A living thing that can never die or be killed.

Legend
A story that has grown up around a heroic figure (who may have been a real person), or an event that may have actually taken place.

Muslim
A follower of Islam, the religion begun by the prophet Mohammed.

Philistine
Philistine is the Arab word for the Palestinians, who have fought the Jews over Palestine since Biblical times.

Prophet or Prophetess
Someone who can tell what happens in the future.

Ritual
A set of holy actions that form part of religious worship. Many important events in our lives are marked by rituals.

Common rituals include weddings for marriage, and funerals for death.

Sacred
The most important parts of religion, or anything that is holy.

Sacrifice
A RITUAL offering to a god or goddess to thank them for their help, or to ask for their support. In the ancient world, the gift was often a human or animal victim.

Sorcerer
Another word for a magician, usually male.

Soul
The part of a creature that thinks and feels. Ancient peoples believed that the soul was IMMORTAL, and that when a person or creature died, their soul went to heaven or the UNDERWORLD.

Spirit
A living being that has no body. Spirit can also mean the SOUL of a creature.

Underworld
The home of dead SOULS, thought by some peoples, such as the Egyptians, to be a land below the earth. Other peoples, such as the Congo of West Africa, believed it was a land that faced downward.

WHO'S WHO

Here's a guide to the hottest names in African and Middle Eastern myths and legends. Names in capitals, for example GENIES, have their own entry.

Adam and Eve (*below*)
According to the Bible, Adam and Eve were the first people ever. They lived in the Garden of Eden, a perfect place for lazing about and eating juicy fruit. There was only one catch — they weren't allowed to eat from the tree of good and evil. But one day, a smooth-talking serpent tempted Eve to take a nibble. She then offered some to Adam. God was so furious he banished the pair to the outside world, where they had to work hard just to survive.

Allah (*al-lah*)
Muslims believe in a single, all-powerful God, called Allah.

Ananse (*a-nan-say*)
Ananse is Mr. Spider, the great trickster god of western Africa. In one story, he is saved from a forest fire by leaping into the ear of an antelope. To say thanks, he later saves the antelope's baby from hunters by weaving a thick web to hide it.

Anubis (*ah-noo-biss*)
This jackal-headed Egyptian god leads dead souls to the world of spirits.

Atum-Ra (*ah–tum rah*) The ancient Egyptian sun god. He rises each day and blazes across the sky in his boat (*above left*). At night, he rests while his boat sails through the land of the dead.

Azazel (*a-za-zell*)
In Arab myth, Azazel is king of the GENIES and leads a rebellion against heaven. In Jewish myth, he teaches humans banned subjects like forging weapons and make-up. When YAHWEH (the Jewish god) finds out, he buries Azazel alive.

Cain and Abel
The Bible tells how Cain was a farmer, and his younger brother, Abel, a shepherd. God looked at their work and liked Abel's meat much more than Cain's vegetables. The jealous Cain killed his younger brother and was cursed by God, just like his mom and dad, ADAM and EVE.

Ga-gorib (*ga-gor-rib*)
According to the Khoi people of southwest Africa, Ga-gorib, the "stone-thrower," sat on the edge of a pit and dared men to throw stones at him. The stones always bounced back, knocking the thrower down into the pit. Finally, the magician hero Heitsi managed to distract the monster and tumbled him into the pit with a well-aimed throw.

Genies (*above left*)
According to Muslim myth, genies were created from the hot winds of the Sahara Desert. They appear as monstrous people or in the shape of jackals, lions, scorpions, or wolves. They also have great magical powers over human beings.

Gilgamesh (*gil-ga-mesh*)
The story of Gilgamesh was written down 4,000 years ago by the Babylonians. Heroic Gilgamesh searches for the secret of eternal life. After a fight, he becomes best friends with the wild man Enkidu (*en-key-doo*). Together they have many adventures — they even wrestle with a bull sent down by ISHTAR's father to bring chaos to Gilgamesh's kingdom (*top*).

Hare
This trickster appears in tales from all over Africa. In one story, Moon sent it to tell

humans that, like the Moon, they will live again the next day when they die. But Hare gets the words mixed up and humans miss their chance to live forever. When she finds out, the angry Moon beats Hare on the head, giving it the split nose it has to this day.

Horus (*hore-us*)
The son of ISIS and OSIRIS (*bottom*), falcon-headed Horus is the Egyptian god of the rising sun.

Hyena
According to the Sudanese people of eastern Africa, sorcerers use hyenas to travel by night. Other peoples believe that the glowing spirits of the dead can be seen in their eyes.

Ishtar (*ish-tar*)
The Babylonian goddess of love and war was famous for her violent nature, her long beard, and her chariot pulled by seven lions. When GILGAMESH said he didn't love her, she got her father to send a bull to destroy his kingdom.

Isis (*eye-sis*)
The Egyptian mother-goddess got her power with a trick. ATUM-RA had grown old, and dribbled in his sleep. Isis mixed his spit with earth to form a snake. When this bit ATUM-RA, Isis said she would cure him only if he told her his secret, magical name. He had no choice, and this secret made her the most powerful goddess.

Kalunga (*cah-loon-gah*)
The supreme god of the Ndonga people of eastern Africa is so enormous that most of him is hidden by mist and cloud as he strides above the hills. Kalunga is also the name for the underworld kingdom where the spirits of the dead live.

Karina (*car-ree-nah*)
In Arab myth, this demon got her magic powers by eating her children. She ruined crops with a single glance, and anyone that looked at her fell ill.

Khadir (*ha-dear*)
An ancient Arab god, named "the Green One," Khadir belongs to a time when the desert was green and fertile. He wanders the globe, visiting the same spot every 500 years.

Kujata (*koo-jah-tah*)
In Arab myth, Kujata is a huge bull with 4,000 eyes, ears, nostrils, and mouths. On its back is a rock of ruby, and on this stands an angel, whose shoulders support the world.

Marduk (*mar-duck*)
The chief god of ancient Babylon, who fought and destroyed the sea monster TIAMAT, cut up her body, and used it to create the universe.

Methuselah (*meth-use-e-lah*)
According to the Bible, Methuselah was the oldest person ever — 969 years old!

Moses (*mo-zez*)
In the Bible, Moses was brought up by the Egyptian royal family after he was found floating in a basket (*top*). When he grew up, he led the Jews back to their homeland in Israel, escaping the Egyptians when God created a path through the Red Sea. On the way, Moses was given the Ten Commandments from God. This set of laws told the Jews how to live.

Nasruddin (*nas-rood-deen*)
This trickster was made up by Arab teachers to test their students. In one story, Nasruddin rode past a customs official every day carrying bags of straw on a donkey. He got richer every trip, but the official couldn't work out what he was selling. When he asked, Nasruddin replied, "Donkeys, of course!"

Ngai (*n-guy*)
To the Masai people of eastern Africa (*bottom*), Ngai is the top god and lives on Mount Kenya. When a Masai is born, Ngai is said to place a guardian angel at their side. He punishes the wicked by striking them with lightning.

Nut (*noot*)
Nut is the Egyptian goddess of the night sky. Her husband is Geb, the Earth god, and her children are ISIS, OSIRIS, and Set.

Osiris (*oh-sire-is*)
The Egyptian god who was said to have taught the Egyptians how to farm. He judges the souls of the dead in the spirit world.

Tiamat (*tee-ah-mat*)
According to the Babylonians, Tiamat (*below right*) was the monster of chaos and salt water. She was mother of the first gods, but because her children were so noisy, she tried to kill them. After a great struggle, she was finally destroyed by MARDUK.

Tortoise (*above left*)
Tortoise is a popular hero in African stories. In one tale, it is caught by Lion. Thinking fast, it tells the Lion that it will taste better once it has been put in water to soften up its shell. Then Tortoise swims to safety!

Tsui' goab (*choi-go-ab*)
A rain god of the Khoi people of southern Africa. His name means "wounded knee," after an injury he got fighting the evil god Gaunab.

Tule (*too-lay*)
Tule is another African spider god who enjoys playing tricks on people.

Yahweh (*yah-way*)
An ancient Jewish name for their single, all-powerful God.

INDEX

*The main stories for each name have page numbers in **bold***

Adam and Eve 29
Aladdin 3, **6–7**, 23
Ali Baba 3, **14–15**, 23
Allah 29
Ananse 29
Anubis 29
Ark 15, 16
Asante 10
Assassins 15
Atum-Ra 29, 30
Azazel 29

Badr-al-Budur 6–7
Bhima 21

Cain and Abel 29

Dagon 21
David **4–5**
Delilah **20–21**
druids, Celtic 11
Dunyazade **23**

Enkidu 30

floods **16–17**

Ga-gorib 29
Gaunab 31
Geb 31
genies 6, **29**
Gilgamesh 30
gods and goddesses 8, 15, 18, 19, 21, 28, **29–31**
Goliath 4–5
Gongola River 11–12

Hare 30
Heitsi 29
Hopi 16
Horus 30

Ibn Battuta 26
Ishtar 30
Isis 3, **8–9**, 30, 31
Israelites **4–5**, 20

Jaliya 10–11
Jesse 4
Jonah 12

Kalunga 30
Karina 30
Khadir 30
Khufu 9
Kujata 31

lions 18, 19
Little Man 12–13

Marduk 31
Merlin 13
Methuselah 31
Milon 20
Mohammed 28
Morgana 14–15
Moses 31
Mount Ararat 17

Nasruddin 31
Ngai 31
Nile River 9
Noah 3, **16–17**
Nut 31
Nyavirezi 18–19

Osiris **8–9**, 30, 31

Palestine 28
passwords 14
Philistines 4, 20, **28**
prophets and prophetesses 28
Puss-in-Boots 15

roc 26

Samson **20–21**
Set **8–9**, 31
Shahriala 22–23
Shariar 22–23
Sheba 24–25
Sheherezade 22–23
shepherds 5
Sinbad 3, 23, **26–27**
slings 4, 5
Solomon **24–25**
sorcerers 6, 7, 28, **30**

Tiamat 31
Timbuktu 7
Tortoise 31
Tsui' goab 31
Tule 31

Underworld, the 9, **28**, 30

Wadlow, Robert 4

Yahweh 29, **31**

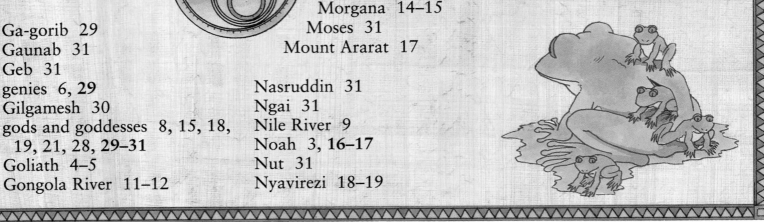